Table of Contents

DEDICATION................................. 3

SEPARATE MONEY AND EMOTIONS 7

IMPORTANCE OF TITHING............. 19

MONEY IS A TOOL......................... 25

THE RIGHT START......................... 37

DEBT GRIND................................ 47

SAVE AND PAY FIRST

BEFORE YOU GET IT..................... 57

THE BIGGEST OBSTACLES............ 73

ACKNOWLEDGEMENTS............... 83

REFERENCES................................ 87

Money Secrets Unveiled

DEDICATION

This book is dedicated to members of all of my families. First to my wife Antoinette, whom I love: and who is a constant reminder to me of beauty and success.

To all of my children: Jenee, Rich, Ebony, Katesha, Azaveus, and David. May these thoughts concerning money add value to your life and bring you success.

To our grandchildren: Bria, our first-born, Angel my favorite grandson, and to Jenelle, Miss Chocolate. If you will adhere to the writings in this book and seek to learn new ways in dealing with money, you can achieve financial success more than any generation before you.

To our godchildren: Zoe, Zion, and Gracie, Here in lies the secrets to your success in life. Use these principles and watch yourselves excel.

To all of my brothers and sisters: May you find in this book something to help guide you the rest of your days upon the earth.

To my man of God, Apostle Norbert Simmons, for your undying support; of entrepreneurs and your always encouraging, attitude. Thank you for being my friend. May God continue to rain down favor on you and First Lady Gwen. You said it was better than money.

To my church family: My prayer is that God will open your spiritual eyes that you might see what His will is for you concerning money. And that He will bless you immensely when you are guided by his principles.

To all who shall lay eyes on this book may it bring you success, beyond what you ever expected, in this lifetime.

RELAFORD / MONEY SECRETS / 6

SEPARATE MONEY AND EMOTIONS

We are humans with emotions and feelings, which are inherent in our natural make-up. There is also inherent in us the ability to think. Truth be known, there is no way to separate these God installed mechanisms, from our being. How then is the way should we deal with it?

There is another mechanism within us, which gives us the ability to determine which has priority at any given time, be it our emotions or rational thinking. That is the freedom of choice. Keep in mind that we need both of these properties to be a part of our natural make up. However, it doesn't mean that they are in harmony with each other. In fact, the opposite is the case. They are always opposed to each other. No need to be alarmed at this point, this is natural because our emotions are the first thing we experience.

As babies, we are used to getting our way. Parents really do not have a choice at this stage in our lives. When we are hungry, they feed us, when wet they change our diaper and on and on. As our need become more demanding, our parent(s) is compelled to meeting them. Let us fast forward to the conflict period.

It is when we reach that time in our lives when the requirements to take on more of the responsibility for ourselves, that the conflict arises. Going from getting what we want to making a choice about which to do, or what to do, can be a daunting task. However we must make a choice. My purpose is to deal with money so let's talk about it.

As with anything in life we deal with, we have to come to grips with it and have an understanding of how to handle it. Once we understand that money answers the very needs of our physical existence, we must make a choice as to what we do with it. It is the very choice itself we have to make, that can be that daunting task. How we choose to deal with it is the key to success or failure. The issues of our lives will most definitely help to shape our choices.

This is true in each generation. However, in today's society the pressure to be or stay in vogue is tremendous. The conflict caused by this pressure can certainly and often does cause problems. Problems within ourselves and with those individuals who love us and care for us most of the time do surface. What we think may be hidden soon comes to the forefront by our actions. The choices or decisions we make reveal us.

Some of the biggest challenges today are technological advances in every area of our society. Cellular telephones, ipads and tablets, kindles, and similar items, and the latest items across the spectrum, give rise to this conflict in our ability to choose.

In yester year there was the" party lines" in the telephone industry. In that day, three different households shared one telephone line for making and receiving calls. Ease dropping was common, where one could carefully pick up the receiver on their phone and listen to the neighbors as they enjoyed a conversation with someone: then there was the one line per household that eliminated ease dropping, but did little to stop the gossip connection.

Now there are cell phones. We can make and receive calls on demand. It seems that everyone in the family has one, if they can understand how to use it. Who would have thought that you could compose a letter and the person you wrote to could get it instantly. Hello texting, email and other means of file sharing. How is it that the world is at our fingertips? The internet, WI-FI, and cloud applications make this possible. Want to read a book without the weight of it, take a picture without a bulky camera, consider a kindle or an ipad or tablet. All of these conveniences come to bear on the choices we make concerning our money. But choose we must.

Want the latest version of these items mentioned above? The array of gadgets changes all the time; we have to ask ourselves do we need the latest version all the time. There are many things that could be mentioned here but my point is to show that there is always a demand on our money. What do you do?

Back to the choices: We must always choose between the two opposing forces built into our human being, feelings or emotions, or rational thinking, to make the best choice the situation demands. Desire which is tied to your emotions, will most of the time, outweigh the need to save money. The rational thinker in you has to overcome desire, because your understanding of the need to save money is more important than the desire to have other things.

Speaking of other things, it seems just about every time there is a family gathering, for Thanksgiving, Christmas, or some other family function there are those of us that always want to go shopping. It is a cancer that eats away at the very fiber of our finances. Usually it is not planned. We were first born with that impulsiveness. Spend, spend, spend is the thought of the moment. Have we considered how much money we have to work with back at home? How much money did we have when we left home? Were all the bills paid? Sometimes we haven't considered how much money we have left for gas to get back home. Have you ever had to borrow money to get back home? Did an emergency occur that you needed money that you didn't have; a car break down, a costly repair, someone got sick and had to go to the emergency room? All of these things must be taken into account.

Remember, just because we leave home doesn't mean that our responsibilities end. When the visit or trip is over; we must return home to face the proverbial music. It is not important to pretend that 'you got all that' to the detriment of your family finances. Don't try to convince others that you have arrived; spending like your money supply is endless. It can turn into some of your biggest headaches. Common sense should tell us that not everyone is in the same situation financially. So there is no need to make believe for the sake of looking good to others. Be honest and know that others understand, and keep what little money you do have.

We are too casual in our attitude toward these things. We must understand that things do and often does happen. Just because we experience good fortune on occasion, doesn't negate the planning we must do to have these situations covered. A well thought out plan that has funding provided, will go a long way in helping to keep the monies you do have available. It will also help you manage your money better. If you follow the plan, the need to borrow money, can be eliminated.

Think about it this way: A family gathering is not a time to shop. They are to catch up on the latest happenings in the family. Introduce the newest members of the family. To fellowship, eat, and enjoy the blessings that God has allowed the family to obtain. When one part of the family is blessed, it should give hope that all can be blessed, if the pattern of saving is followed. Don't let the emotion of jealousy take a prominent role here. It is easy to be envious of the success, or seeming success of others. Their success or seeming success should make you get close enough to them to learn some of their secrets of how they did it. Any successful person will be glad to tell you how they achieved what they have, just be willing to listen and try it for yourself. Believe me, you shouldn't be surprise that someone knows something that you don't know. Shared experiences can play a key role in getting started in the right direction.

As I wrote this chapter, I noticed a statement via, the world, wide, web, by a company in the financial industry. "They recommended starting a family tradition of savings". I concur, and whole-heartedly believe that saving is a primary way of meeting future financial needs and goals.

IMPORTANCE OF TITHING

Let me first make some comments concerning this thing, called tithing. It is my strong belief that tithing is right in every aspect of the financial spectrum: Personal income, business income, and other sources of money you receive. What I mean is; that if money is finances and it takes money to make up a financial portfolio and we are going to have lasting success with that financial portfolio, then we have to recognize God as the source of not just money, but of all things pertaining to what we have. It is, He who allows us to receive and obtain the money that we have. The bible states that 'He has made all things for Himself'.

That includes us as humans and what we think, or how we receive what is written, has no bearing on the truth of His word. Therefore, I choose to believe tithing is a way to recognize God as the giver and sustainer of our very existence.

In believing that tithing is right and doing it, says I recognize the truth of God's word. What is His word regarding tithing? I am glad you asked. He said, and I paraphrase, "If we tithe, examine and see if He will not stay or stop the hand of the devourer; that which comes to hinder or to take away what He has predestined for you to have in the way of money". So then begs' the question, what is the tithe?

The tithe according to the bible is the tenth. Webster, that great definer of words for the modern world, also defined the tithe as the tenth. What then is the tenth? The tenth of all increases in monies that comes into our possession for our personal use is the tithe. That potion represents the tenth part of what we get. It comes from the gross amount of monies that is received. That is the amount before any governmental institutions; whether federal, state or local has made any deductions from it. It is, not based on the net portion. It is ten percent as we learned in math. If it is not ten percent then it is not a tithe, and it does not honor God: and nor does God regard it as a tithe.

How then should tithe be, handled? The first tenth of all we get goes to God. It is important to separate the tenth before we designate where the first penny is going. Once we do this, we have made the first step in honoring God. Moreover, we recognize it is, He who gives us the ability and the strength and the mind to get wealth. This says to Him, we are not able to do anything on our own except He gives us the strength.

It is through our local church God has set up for the tithe to be, placed. Once we place the tithe there, we have completed the process in honoring God with the money we make. Understand that when you give the tenth it belongs to God and it is not yours. So avoid making statements like, I paid my tithe. That potion that you acquired is not yours. It is His. When you tithe, you honor God for every aspect of your life. He in turn takes care of His end of the deal, according to His word. When the first tenth is in place, then what you have left is yours to do as you please. Be careful not only in how you use it; moreover, be careful in what you call it, or how you view it. What do I mean? Some have said that when you give God the first tenth that you have the other ninety percent to yourself.

I have come to the understanding that if the first tenth belongs to God, it was not yours to begin with, so it could not be that you have the other ninety percent. We can't count anything until we separate God's portion. Then it is true that what is left is ours. However, I see it as a hundred percent. It is one hundred percent because now it can be considered belonging to you. God allows us to take control over all that remains for our use, after we have separated His. It should seem impossible to call all that is yours only ninety percent. You actually have control of one hundred percent of your money. Think about it. When you say you only have ninety percent, you omit the fact that the first tenth is not yours until His is, separated, and should not be included in your budget. That, in my opinion is faulty logic, and faulty thinking, and should be, avoided at all cost.

Therefore, now that we have a better understanding of tithing, what should be done with the portion you get to keep as your own? Let us explore this question in another chapter, 'The Right Start'.

MONEY IS A TOOL

Proper use of tools, play a major role in the production, performance, and outcome, of any endeavor, whether it be providing products or services. In the general sense of tool usage, tools need to be in good working order, to produce the desired outcome in making a product and providing a service. In order to achieve the best possible results in either category your tools must function properly. Most of us probably never thought of money as being a tool. From our early experience, we learned it could buy things that someone else sold. Usually, it was at the local general, grocery, or convenient store. If we would have had a different concept of money early on, we would have known that we were using our tools improperly. Let us explore this idea further.

During early childhood money as a tool never entered our minds. For the most part neither did it enter the minds of our parents. If it had, they would have made us realize we were wasting and destroying the very tools we needed throughout life. Sure a trip to the store, whichever one did not matter, it made us happy.

Whenever, we got some money the first thought in our mind was to run down to the local store. Those old timey candies and cookies, and those big RC colas, grape and orange sodas, just thrilled us to no end. Those were happy times in our lives, but as we starved for the pleasures of the day, unbeknownst to us we were jeopardizing the potential of our future.

As we journey through life, we encounter others who know more about money than we do. I met such a person in one named, Apostle Norbert Simmons, who is the founding pastor of Deeper Life Church Ministries, who is consistent in teaching that money is a tool and should be viewed and used as such. He is an advocate for those who are and those who aspire to become entrepreneurs.

He was the owner of a thriving produce business before the Lord called him into fulltime ministry. With his enthusiastic support when I asked him in early June of 2000, if he thought it was too late to start a lawn service business. He said no; and told me to go for it. Since then, my wife and I have been successful in that business for more than thirteen years. We value his experience and expertise, and his spiritual insight.

We recommend to anyone, to always have a man or woman of God you can trust in, and rely upon, to give you a relevant word and sound wisdom for your endeavors.

One day at a board of directors meeting at my local church, I asked Mr. Sol Hicks, who is a multi-millionaire, was the top producer at Prudential Insurance Company for more than ten years, if he would give me one thought, about money off the top of his head. He stated that, "money has a spirit and you have to respect it. If it is not respected it goes away from those who do not respect it. And it goes to those who know how to respect it". As I thought about what he said, it sums up what I am writing about in this book.

Getting back to money as a tool, I taught my favorite niece that money is a tool and you always need to have tools in your toolbox, your savings account.

As we progress through each stage in life, the need to have the tools you should, grows rapidly as we age. Our desires grow with each passing year, and place a demand on the tools in the tool chest; provided we have placed anything in there.

Another point to mention here is that an early start beats fast running. So get started early placing tools in your chest. Along with desires and needs as we get older, the things we need or want gets more and more costly. This should drive us to place more and more tools in the toolbox. Therefore, some creativity in producing more tools is necessary and helpful as we go. If we placed our money in the toolbox, this would give increase to our tool chest.

Doctor Benjamin Carson in his book 'America the Beautiful' asked a question. "Have you ever stopped to think about what money represents? His answer was it represents wealth and power. He went on to say when you lack money and incur debt, your influence and power decrease".

As mentioned, our first instinct, when we got money, was to head to the store. Instead, of spending, what would it be like, if we loaded that money into our tool chest? The smallest amounts of money we get are our true test of our ability to manage. In managing our money we have to place money in the proper perspective. The little amounts we get should be dealt with properly from the beginning. This will determine what we do with larger amounts. The biggest mistake most people make is to think the little amounts do not matter. If this is your view, you are well on the way to financial missteps. That will be your ruin if that view is not changed. The little matters greatly because what is done with the little; is the beginning of establishing habits of what you will do with any amount, large or small.

Initially, as we start out what we receive are usually small amounts of money that come our way. Normally, what we get, is given to us by family, or friends, or someone, being nice to us. Most of the time it's in dominations of the coin variety; pennies, nickels, dimes, occasionally, quarters, fifty cents pieces, but rarely a coin dollar, but it sometimes does happens.

Interestingly, only six coins comprise the American Monetary System. The rest of the American Monetary System is comprised of paper bills. They are one, five, ten, twenty, fifty, and hundred dollar bills. There are six coins and six bills.

As we grow and age, our money starts coming through different sources: from an allowance, if you are fortunate enough to have parents, who are able to reward you, for doing your chores, from a job you were able to get, or from an inheritance or some other source like a business you own. Whether we are talking about the coins or the paper bills, each denomination is important.

As you save, the larger the amount that you put into your tool chest, the stronger your tools become. The strength of your tools determines the type of activities you'll be able to engage in. Perhaps you want to take a trip, buy clothes, a bike, a car, a house, land etc. The size and strength of your toolbox will determine what you will be able to accomplish. So put lots of tools into your toolbox.

In putting tools into your toolbox, there are some things to keep in mind as you do so. You will want to protect your investment. Why call it an investment?

What you have saved, you have earned. Jack Benny once said, "A penny saved is a penny earned". How true is that statement? I believe it is very correct to say that, because if you never save it, then where is it! In saying that, your earnings, must be something you can realized. In other words, show me where you saved it, and then you have earned it. If you cannot show it, then you have not earned it. To protect your investment here is what I recommend.

Put a freeze on your credit. Yes, freeze it. I do not mean putting it in the freezer. What you do is simply request to each credit-reporting agency not to allow information contained in your files to be, given out to anyone who is requesting it. You are assigned a protective code only you will be able to use to unfreeze, or thaw your credit file. When you want your credit files to be available for whatever reason, you just simply thaw it for a time. Once the reason for thawing is complete, then you refreeze it.

Freezing your credit file does some amazing things. It helps to prevent identity theft from occurring. If someone is trying to access your report, they cannot because they do not have the code that only you have. This prevents someone from opening accounts in your name. In addition, it stops creditors from viewing your credit file to make you an offer of credit. This in turn helps to protect your credit score by reducing inquiries into your credit history, which can hurt your score. I learned this effective technique of credit freezing from listening to the Clark Howard radio program.

THE RIGHT START

As mentioned in the chapter on tithing, let us look at what we do with the money that is ours after we give God His.

Imagine if we had saved all of the money we received since we were a child or when we first got money. How much would you have right now? What would be the value of your tool chest?

One thing, we would be off to a good start depending on our age had we done that. We would be able to buy whatever we desired according to the amount of tools in our chest. While this would be living in a fantasy world, what I am about to tell you is not.

While it would be next to impossible to have saved all of the money we received since we obtained our first coin or bill, it is not impossible to save a percentage of what we get. Its' been said, knowledge is power but I say putting that knowledge to the proper use is more powerful.

Let's take a look at a farmer. The land the farmer is going to plant has to be prepared to receive the seed that will be, planted, in it. Once properly tilled and plowed the seeds are placed in the ground. Depending on the type of seeds, they are, planted, one per hole, or multiple seeds are, planted, in the same hole. Either way the hope is that the land would produce more and more of the seeds that was planted. At harvest time, the farmer must decide on what to do with the crop; that is what the seeds have yielded. Understanding the law of seedtime and harvest, the farmer knows that the harvest is always, greater than, the seeds that were sown.

In dealing with the harvest, the farmer must know how much to use in each area of responsibility. A decision has to be made as to how much should be saved for next year's planting, how much will be used for food, how much will be sold, and what amount should be used to help neighbors.

Just as the farmer, we should all be prepared to determine how much of our earnings are going to be placed in saving for the future, how much will be used for living expenses, and how much will be used to help others. All said, we must be prepared to properly manage our finances.

As we mentioned in the chapter on tithing, a tithe is ten percent. Remember the part that is left after you gave God what belongs to Him? That is the part; I want to deal with at this point.

What is left; to our use is one hundred percent. God has given us a great guideline to go by with the ten percent method He set in place. If He gets ten percent, why not, since you get to determine what happens to your portion, save at least ten percent. Now when you save that percentage, you will have ninety percent left. The amount of money you make should have no bearing on saving the proper amount each time you get paid or receive money. This would guarantee that money will be set aside for your future needs and your desires. This concept is termed pay yourself first. You should always do this before one penny go to anybody or anything. Your life depends on it. If you are to have a future that is satisfied and fulfilled, saving enough money is imperative.

Sorry, your emotions will have to take a back seat to your saving plan. Saving has to be a habit so that you are consistent in doing it, and it becomes second nature, automatic. Avoid using your savings tool chest. Use the other ninety percent. The remaining balance should also be, designated for a specific purpose percentage wise. The other needs in your life should come from the ninety percent but should be a specific percentage amount, as your savings are. I always recommend saving more if it is possible.

A well thought out plan should always be available to review at any time. Such a written plan will help to maintain focus and can be, used to track performance. Your plan must not be limited to just savings. It must include life insurance, auto insurance and, homeowners, insurance. If you rent, your plan should include renters insurance, to cover your valuables against fire, flood or theft, as with other types of insurances. Your plan should also have ample monies to cover expenses such as utilities.

Of upmost importance, your plan must include money for emergencies. They happen usually without warning and can be devastating on finances. If you have children and/or grandchildren, have you included them in your planning? Biblical scholars know that God has commanded that we leave an inheritance for our children's, children. In other word, that means your children and grandchildren. Put yet another way you are actually saving for three generations of your family: yourself, your children and your grandchildren.

This is how my wife and I do it. For each of our children living at home and our grandchildren, we save $8.34 each month. At the end of the year they will have one hundred dollars in their account.

As soon as they are born, and get a social security number, we start their account at the bank. You open an account in the child's name, under the Uniform Gifts to Minor's Act, at the place where you save or bank. Each year they live, deposited in their account is a hundred dollars.

Upon graduation from high school, the first option we give them is; to take over their account. If they take over their account, then we are finished saving for them. At that point they will have to save and maintain their own plan. The second option for them is to let us keep control of their account. If we maintain control of the account, they can spend as they please, as long as they exercise good stewardship over their finances, while we continue to add the monthly deposit into their savings accounts. Even though they choose this second option, they will still have to develop a savings plan of their own to supplement what we are doing. What a joy it is to save for your future generation!

Children that are already outside the home and have not had the opportunity to have a savings account, with us, they will have to rely on their own savings plan. The other option for them is to wait on proceeds from a life insurance policy that you have in place, should one or both parent(s) die.

We are expected to be good stewards over the money we have. So as we go forward, we see that there are numerous demands on the money we have and money we potentially will make in the future. How we handle the money, whether it is in our hands now, or is to come in tomorrow, it is imperative that we plan for its usage.

Today's action will determine tomorrow's outcome. Are you setting the course for your family's future to be bright, and uninhibited by lack of money? Have you given in to your impulsiveness and emotion to take the easy road to having everything you ever wanted right now? Will you be able to avoid the debt grind?

Consider using an income and expense sheet to track your monies received and monies spent. This simple form, if kept up, can give you an instant snapshot of where you are financially. You can develop these forms, using Microsoft programs like excel and access. If you are serious about your family's future, this spread sheet can make all the difference in showing how much money is at your disposal. Then you will have the tool necessary to make any needed adjustments. You can see a sample copy of an income and expense spread sheet at the end of this book.

DEBT GRIND

This an area of life in which we have succumbed to our emotions; and the things that we do or have done were impulsive and not well thought out. In addition to impulsiveness, we have failed to plan and to exercise good judgment over the resources we had and needed. Our desire to have what we want right then, outweighed any rational thinking. As a result, we end up in what I call the debt grind.

The debt grind is a situation in which current and future earnings are, mired in demands from creditors. In addition, we owe our family members, friends, and others, because this is usually how we start borrowing money. Unfortunately, too many of us do not realize the direness of the situation until we are, unable to pay the just debt, we have incurred. Always one more item(s) purchased on credit, will not hurt; that's' because we have not made an effort to assess the financial situation.

To make matters worse, companies know how to appeal to our emotions and are usually successful in getting us to take one more bite of the proverbial credit pie. Because they are so effective at what they do, we never see it coming. They skillfully bait us with schemes and cleverly concocted ways at time in our life when we are most vulnerable. These merchants have mastered extending credit and they do it with such ease on you and me the unsuspecting consumer.

Sure, we get what we want, when we want it, and the creditors are all too glad, to let us have what we want. The amount of interest and hidden fees can be astronomical. Because we feel that we can handle the payments, without ever considering, if we can, we dive head long into another credit situation without counting the cost. We buy clothes, TV's, electronics, cars, boats, trucks, and items we just think we want. All too often, these are things we buy and are not at all, what we need.

The main reason these things are purchased most of the time is because, of impulsiveness. If we stopped to consider whether or not we needed those things, most of the time the answer would be no. The creditors don't control your emotions; however, they influence them, and are glad to assist in this undertaking.

When we meet with creditors, we let then influence us because we have not controlled our impulsiveness. We let them tell us how much we can afford to pay because we only show them the big picture of our finances. In other word we tell them how much money we make overall and we let them tell us, "yes you can afford to pay so much per week or month" base on your income. On occasion, the opposite of the big picture maybe the case we present to the creditor. We sometimes do not divulge our true financial picture. We do this because we want them to say yes and not deny what we want. Most of the times we do not know what the true position of our finances are because of our failure to have a plan. We do this, and have not, considered the amount of money we already have going out or the amount that maybe coming in. You are in the best position to know how much you have to work with. Knowing how much you can afford is a great asset in decision-making. When what they say you can afford exceed a certain dollar amount, you have to be willing to decline the offer and walk away. Your rational thinking will have rescued you from a financial blunder and kept your emotions in check.

As we dive deeper into the debt grind, the inevitable is happening with each passing day, week, month, and year. The amount of money at your disposal is diminishing. There is less money to continue to fuel the irresponsible behavior. One of the first signs that gets our attention is, when we experience a turn down, or denial, by a new or existing creditor, when we apply for credit on another item to satisfy our emotion. However, if we want to purchase something in which the creditor can use it as collateral, such as a car, boat or house, the interest rate to borrow that money now becomes very high. The rate is normally higher than that of a person with normal, responsible borrowing ability. That is borrowing within your ability to repay the loan.

The spiral of the debt grind continues as our inability to pay back creditors, moves to them calling and demanding their money. If these payments continues to be delinquent, then you are reported to one of the three credit reporting agencies (Experian, Equifax and Transunion) making it tougher for you to have credit extended to you. In today's society the ramifications of bad debt is far more detrimental than previous times in our history. One of the most alarming is; it can affect your ability to get a job or open a bank account. The stakes are high so get your emotions in check early and keep them in check. Additionally, when you become a credit risk, and with this status, you will always be denied for any new request for credit.

For every negative report by someone your have failed to pay, that have been reported to one of the credit agencies, seven years have been determined by law, to impact your ability to secure new borrowing. A word of advice at this point; if you have reached this level of irresponsibility, it may be wise not to pay any more money on one or more bills that are delinquent. Currently the law supports this position. If you are unable to pay it completely off, then paying anything extends the date when the seven years end. This results in your credit situation going longer than seven years.

Your goal, given the above-mentioned situations should be, not to engage in any new credit obligations. Resist the urge to continue in the spiral of disenchantment and delusion. Always keep in the forefront of your mind that the reason you are in this kind of situation, is because of irrational behavior and unchecked emotions. This is another situation where you have to put you feelings and unbridled emotions on lockdown. You have to grit your teeth, if you have too, and let rational thoughts take the forefront. It may seem as if you are hurting yourself, but you are actually on the road to recovery.

An old Mexican man, said to me, "that things are always hard before they get easy." The bad news is that he is right. It is hard. However, the good news is, he is also right when he said it becomes easy. Out of the dimness of the moment just know that things are getting better for you. It is because you then have allowed the right start to be rekindled in your financial decisions.

Dire situations call for unusual actions. If an emergency arises, unless you have put aside funds to handle it, then you risk not being able to cope with the emergency. Your standard of living starts to be substandard. Money for children, if you have them, is scarce and hard to come by. Places like check into cash, payday loans, and loan sharks, can become a way of life.

When items purchased with borrowed money begin to lose their value, what is the alternative to replace them? What happens to your liberty and freedom you once enjoyed? How will your relationship, with those, you love or those who love you be affected? Will you be able to settle for being without, or having second best or welfare for a choice? Are you or will you be prepared to handle the negative impact of the debt grind?

SAVE AND PAY FIRST BEFORE YOU GET IT

The first time I heard someone say anything about money was Ms. Anna. When I was old enough to comprehend words, I heard her say "Y'all save your money". This was a constant theme in our home from her, as I recall. With twelve children to nurture and feed, I wondered, as I got older, was she saving any money. What she said, always stuck with me. Like many others, I let my emotions get the best of me, and my money. What I just said, is an understatement, grossly misrepresented. The truth of the matter is I did not have any money. Mom always managed to save what she could, for my siblings and me, mostly for the one who needed money the most. Being that middle child among the children my needs did not seem to matter, compared to the older children. However, she always managed to get her priorities right. Although mom has passed on, I can still hear her say, "Y'all save your money".

Savings is key and paramount to anyone's financial future. Multi-millionaire, Al Williams, once stated, "It's not, how much you make but it's, how much you keep". He was the founder and President of Primerica Life Insurance Company. What a well-stated assessment! He went on to say, "We make a lot of money in a life time but how much we keep is more important". I happen to subscribe to this philosophy. I believe a consistent savings plan will help you reach your financial goals during your lifetime.

As I grew up and started taking jobs, my desires started to drive my motivation. There were those things I wanted, that I thought of as a child. My first big-ticket item I wanted was a car. I was sixteen at the time. I wanted to be able to drive myself to school during my junior and senior years in high school. When my brother, two years my senior, who always thought he deserved more respect than he thought he received, left for the army, he left his Chevy Chevelle home that I could drive. So I started driving it to school.

We lived twenty miles from where we went to high school. I had a problem with timing how long it took me to get to school. I had been late a few times, and the principle told me if I was late again he was going to suspend me from school. So one day I was running late and decided not to check the oil in the car. I was about five miles from school when the car started making a clacking noise. Not long after that, it quit running. I was late for school and suffered the consequences.

Mom told me if I saved my money, she would take me to get a car. Therefore, I looked in the want ads in the Savannah Morning News, our local newspaper and found a car I could afford. It was a 1968 Ford Galaxy 500 fastback style car. It listed for $550.00. I had saved a little more than that so Ms. Anna, as agreed, took me to pick up the car. That was my first vehicle I purchased at the age of seventeen, and paid cash for it! Since then, I have had many cars. Probably, way too many; they can become, and often do, a hole to put money in never to see that money again.

In 1975 after graduating from high school, I moved away from home to Brunswick, Georgia. It was only a forty five minute drive, but it was away from home. It was short lived. I quickly grew tired of the daily routine of wasting my life and time not doing anything constructive. It was at that point I knew I needed to do something else.

In pursuit of making this change, I decided to join the US Air Force. After meeting, all the necessary requirements, I was accepted into the Air Force. However, there is one thing I should mention here. After doing a background check, my recruiter shared with me something I did not know. He told me had I gotten one more traffic ticket of any type, I would not have been able to join the military. That would have crushed me because I always wanted to go to the Air Force. At least the smart ones if they join any branch it would be the Air Force.

After joining, I set my sight on staying with the Air Force for four years. During this time, I thought I would settle down, gain some experience, see the world, make good use of my time, and save some money. I was successful at all but saving money. This aspect of my tenure seemed to elude me. The fun I was having, cause my emotions to get the best of me. All it seemed of my rational thinking was that, it was a mist. When my four years was ending I realized, I had not accomplished the savings I envisioned.

Not wanting to separate after four years, because I had failed to save, made me re-think my decision, so I decided to re-enlist for another four years. I sort of did not learn from my first four years. During my second four year stint, I was still doing all things I set out to do, except, you guessed it, save! After re-enlisting several, more times I ended up doing twenty years more than I intended to do. Better late than never is a slogan I can really relate too.

After marrying my lovely wife Antoinette, I actually came to grips with savings. Until I met and married her, I only had a desire to save. She also had a desire to save and would. Actually witnessing her actions caused me to be motivated to put into practice something that had eluded me for so many years of my life. Something triggered my motivation that made me become more serious about saving.

When it was official we were getting married, I did not want to be, accused of, or have her say in our latter years, that we never went on a honeymoon. That is when I decided to test my resolve to save. Long story short I did it. I decided I would take her on a cruise for our honeymoon. On October 3, 2004, we boarded a flight to Ft Lauderdale Florida, and the next day we set sail to Key West, Florida and Cozumel, Mexico. I booked that cruise early enough, to get the very first suite on the port side of the cruise ship, The Fascination. Oh, what a wonderful time we had! Our honeymoon was fascinating to say the least.

When we returned, everything from the airline flight, the cruise ship, the off shore excursions, the return flight, to Raleigh-Durham International, was paid in full and we had money left. All of these expenses was paid in cash.

Since our beginning, we have had many, many more trips of various kinds. We have flown to Philadelphia, Miami, Boston, Los Angeles, Seattle, San Antonio, New Orleans, and Dallas Forth Worth. We have taken the breath taking, Alaskan Cruise, and cruised the beautiful, Bahamas. In addition to these flight and cruises, we have taken other trips to places we drove ourselves.

In 2009 for Antoinette's birthday, we traveled to Orlando, Florida, purchased her a 2004 Mercedes E500, with less than 50,000 miles on it, and were paid, in full, using cash. We were able to pay cash because we saved the money we needed to purchase this vehicle. Antoinette and I both worked. We saved together. The accounts we have are set up according to how we want to use them. That is for a specific purpose. We do not have separate secret individual accounts. We did all of these things in less than ten years. The exciting part is that we have never borrowed any money of any kind, from anyone, or any financial institutions to assist us in these travels and numerous other purchases we have made.

There was an existing mortgage, on the house, I had, prior to us getting married but we sold that house, and bought a new house and carried a mortgage on it. A word on that: we both had credit problems after going through divorce. We will explain credit problems in the next chapter.

Under the save and pay first method the idea is to pay cash for your purchases. For instance, let us say you wanted a car that cost $20,000. The question is how long do you want to finance the car; how many months? That is the exact question; you would get at the dealership if you were to borrow the money, which would be financing the vehicle. However, you are not going to borrow the money. You save the money on your own before you buy the car. If you saved for 36 months, you would have to save approximately $555 for each of those months. If you wanted a lower payment, which is a choice when you borrow, you choose a longer payment period. For instance, on 48 months, you would have to save $416. The beauty of this method is there are no finance charges to borrow money because you will be saving your own. If you borrowed $20,000 and financed it using simple financing you would incur an additional $1000 at five percent interest. Your monthly payment would be $583 for 36 months. If you borrowed the money and defaulted on the payments, you would jeopardize having the car repossessed. If you were saving on your own and had to miss a payment for some reason, there would be no penalty. You could always continue when you were able. Saving before you purchase poses no problems with your credit rating.

Using this method assumes you are too young to own a car, or you already have one. This would be ideal because you have a way to get around while you save. If you are too young to own a vehicle right now, perhaps your parents or someone is going to give you one, or be generous enough to let you drive one they own, until you are old enough or get your own.

Once you have saved and purchased the vehicle or item you want, it is yours free and clear of any leans on it. That is a great way to get a jump on your finances. What do I mean?

The money that you would be spending on the purchase of a vehicle or other items would be going directly to your savings and other designated accounts as you choose. You would have demonstrated to yourself you can save for what you want and would have developed a good habit concerning money. As you get older, you would have more tools to work with as you start thinking about bigger venues. At this point, you would have done a great favor to yourself and your children's children. You get control of your emotions and impulses, and you employ the use of your rational thinking.

To further expound on my reason for writing this book we are among the biggest givers at our local church, Deeper Life Church Ministries, and proud of it. We do believe that our giving along with our savings have propelled us to a place neither of us ever dreamed possible.

All of what I said in the preceding paragraphs is a result of what I call, save and pay first. After you have followed these procedures, everything is a done deal.

You do not owe anybody, any banks, or credit unions, any money. So when it is all said and done, you come out on top, a winner, and all the better financially.

We have had many more projects, including home improvements, and other things that I have not mentioned here that we have paid for using cash. The bottom line is; we have done it because our mind was set towards reaching our set goals.

THE BIGGEST OBSTACLES

To begin with, the biggest obstacle will be you. Make no mistake, you may blame something or someone, however, you will be the biggest culprit to gaining a financial foothold on your future.

The pressure of the times in which we live, will cause your emotions to want to take precedence over just about everything you do. Being in vogue and having the latest fads, fashions and frills can sometimes over take us unawares. Before we know it, we are doing what everyone else is doing and as a result, we can lose focus, on what is, important. Avoid using you hard- earned money for things that are not important to your overall goals. Remember the reason for your goals!

Something else comes to mind as we journey through life. Do we borrow or save for what we want? Since we as humans most of the time, desire to take the easy way, borrowing will seem the logical thing to do. Here is a word of caution! Thinking you have to or need to borrow is faulty logic. Rest assured your emotions have gotten the best of you and have overtaken your sense of reasoning, if you think you need to borrow. Saving would be the logical thing to do. It will seem hard because it put your impulsiveness on hold and makes it wait. Waiting is something that breaks down the wagon of progress, as far as we are concerned. However, you must know and realize that logic and reasoning must win here, for you to have a better future. Your future is more important!

Family and friends can be helpful if they are positive. Too often, they can be a negative influence because what you are attempting to do they are not familiar with the process. Neither have most of your friends done it before. If this were the case, there will, without hesitation be, some reluctance on their part, to support your savings plan. They will try to convince you to take the easy route, thinking they are helping you. You need to remember, the easy way will get you there faster. It will not only get you the things you want faster but it will get you into debt fast as well. Avoid the debt grind!

Easy to get money will find you. Banks and finance companies will certainly try to entice you into taking money from them in hopes of making more at your expense. They will pitch you lines like; you have excellent credit, you can get anything you want, you can have this amount on your signature alone and many other tactics to get you to bend. Keep in mind the reason they can offer you money is that they have peeped into your credit by some means and know you are not a credit risk, and you have the ability to pay them back. They want your money with interest. Avoid the temptation!

Softhearted people are the kind of folks everybody seeks out when they need a loan. Especially if you are the type that have used your rational thinking in your dealing with money and know how to put your emotions on hold and save, watch out. They will come to you to separate you from your money. They have good intentions, but do not have your best interest at heart. Usually, they are the type that is controlled by impulses and want you to act hastily and impulsively when they approach you about your money. A firm no should be sufficient. You do not owe them a reason or explanation as to why you denied their request. Avoid irresponsible people!

From the previous chapter we mention the existing mortgage I had before our second marriage. The interest rate on the existing first and second mortgage was nearly twenty-four percent. Since our credit situation has gotten better through time and proper management, we now have an interest rate of two point seven five percent. We say to God be the glory.

To add to our dilemma we had failed to properly act or respond to a letter from the IRS, Internal Revenue Service. This is not revenue from within your house providing you with service. Let me borrow a term from texting. (Lol), laugh out loud. The letter stated that we had improperly filed our taxes in tax year 2009 and owed the federal government over $7,000. They began by garnishing over $400 per paycheck from my wife's wages. As if that was not enough to hurt us, they then started garnishing my wages, which amounted to over $700 per month altogether. All of These actions took place within a seven-month period in 2011.

The actions taken by the IRS put a great deal of pressure on us in meeting our needs and our financial obligations. It hampered us during the time it was taking place. Although, bothered by the garnishment of our wages, we realized we and no one else had failed to respond in a timely manner to the letter from the IRS. When they began to take action, it was too late for us to set up a payment schedule with them.

If you are reading this book now a note of caution, do not ignore correspondence from importance sources. Do not treat these important letters, like junk mail. Failure to act can cause unwanted changes in your life style, you were not expecting.

We learned a very valuable lesson though the actions taken against us. We still managed to pay all of our bills that we had at the time. Then it dawned on us, we still maintain, as the money was garnished; we ought to be able to save even more money. So what was at one time hurting us turned into a mechanism by which we realized we could save more money; we learned from this setback and did exactly that and saved more. What we discovered, was opportunities to save more. Sometimes obstacles can position you for a better future and boost your financial endeavors.

It was through these obstacles and other situations in life that we developed the save and pay first method in dealing with our money.

Feelings and impulsiveness unchecked and uncontrolled will usually wreck your finances.

Moreover, leave you in a restrained position of discomfort and stress.

The rational thinking you, will be the catalyst in helping you to reach your financial goals, and have a bright rewarding future, financially.

ACKNOWLEDGEMENTS

I would like to thank my wife for her efforts in designing the cover page of this book. You did a superb job sweetheart!

Thanks to my son David who supported me as I compiled the materials for this book.

Thanks Sharita for the support you give to Antoinette and me on a regular basis and your work in dealing with the copyrights process.

Thanks to my friends Winston and Carolyn in your help and support throughout the many years since I have existed.

A special thanks posthumously, to Ms. Anna, my mother, for her teaching and guidance and the love she had for all of her children.

Last, but not least thanks to LaQuetta Robinson for her help in proofing this manuscript.

Income	Expense	Balance	Purpose
0	0	0	

References

Carson, B. (2012). *America the beautiful. Rediscovering what made this great nation.* Zondervan, Grand Rapids, Michigan: Library of Congress Cataloging-In Publication. DOI: www.zondervan.com/ebooks

http://www.merriam-webster.com/

www.ingramcontent.com/pod-product-compliance
Lightning Source LLC
Chambersburg PA
CBHW071753170526
45167CB00003B/1014